I'd like to dedicate this book in loving memory of my nephew

Garrett Houston

And my cousin

Tina Taylor

Gone but never forgotten

1

John 3:16

For God so loved the world, that he gave his only begotten Son, that whosoever believeth in him should not perish, but have everlasting life

# Poetry Through

# Heaven

## Courtney R. Houston

## Dusty Bible

Time to make some changes

Time to pick up the dusty bible

My Mamaw always told me

To turn to it when I need the truth

I pull her dusty bible off the shelf

And started to pray

God, please correct me

Don't give up on me

This world keeps getting worse, and worse

Satan has his hands on this world so tight

Christians are getting bashed

Time to dust off the bible

And get back on track

# The Storm

The rain will pour

The waves will crash

The enemy will push you down

You'll hear the sound

Of silence pulling you down

As you walk around a town

That you feel lost in

Full of sin

You feel like you'll never be the same

That's part of Satan's game

God will pull you though the storm

As the rain pours

He will soar

Take you places you never been

When you're lost

He will find you

In the storm

He comforts you

The storm is only temporary

Have faith

God will pull you through

## Famous

So many famous people in the world

Big houses, fancy cars

Living this out of control life

Being not who they are

Having a gift

That was given from the Lord above

Don't even have time to say thanks

To the Lord above

To busy being famous

Don't even thank God for the gift

Fancy cars and diamonds

Forget about the King

Gods the only reason your famous

But you don't take the time to say thank you

## On Fire For You

Lord, tonight I'm on fire for you

Yes, I know God your love is true

I know no matter what the battle

I can trust in you

Lord, I'm on fire for your love

Thank you for your blessings

That you sent from above

God you are so amazing

I'm on fire for your love

On fire for you

On fire for you

My soul is on fire

And not the way Satan wants it

Your love is so rewarding

All I want to do is live for you

## My Permanent Home

My permanent home isn't here

It's up above where there are no tears

Here on earth I'll worship him

As a Christian we get lost in sin

Sometimes we lose our way

But our Lord Jesus is never far

He's with you in your car

He's with you in your home

When you feel alone

He's your comfort in the storm

When I get to my permanent home

I will meet loved ones at the gate

Smile bright, and see Jesus face

When I get to my permanent home

I will take Jesus hand

Walk down the road of gold

I will finally be free

When I get there

At my permanent home

## If Heaven Had Face Time

If Heaven had Face time

I'd call you everyday

I'd get to see your smiling face

I learned one thing from you

You have to grab life and embrace

I know you're in a better place

I know that you're safe

But if Heaven had Face time

It wouldn't be so hard

I still wouldn't get to hug you

But I'd still tell you that I love you

Get to see you smile and laugh

Make jokes like we use to

This would all be easy

If Heaven had Face time

## Snowball Fight With Jesus

Garrett, it's been a long morning

Listening to Christmas songs

Looking at the Christmas tree

Wondering what you're doing

Wondering who you'd be

Is the snow falling down up there?

Are you having a snowball fight with Jesus?

Are you walking beside him on the snow covered road?

Is it cold up there?

Like it is down here?

I hope you're happy spreading cheers

It's so sad down here

Are you with Wyatt?

Have you two built a snowman?

Are you both having a snowball fight with Jesus?

Are you singing with the angels?

Have you decorated a Christmas tree?

This Christmas won't be the same down here

Because you're spending Christmas with Jesus this year

Miss you so much

Aunt Cookie loves you

## I'm Going To Fly

Bring on the pressure Satan

Try with your power

My Lord and Savior is with me

He's with me every hour

Nobody is going to stop me from going home

One day, yes one day

I'm going to fly

Fly up in the sky

Walk through the gate with a smile

Sit on the clouds for a while

Talk to my loved ones

That has went before me

I'm going to fly

I'm going to fly

Nobody is going to stop me

## Just Don't Seem Like Christmas

Families everywhere join together with cheer

No, not me

I could barely put up my tree

Just don't seem like Christmas

Now that we lost you

You brought so much joy

You're the angel at the top of my tree

Heaven must be bright tonight

Even though Garrett you are far

You will always remain in our hearts

Just don't seem like Christmas

So many fears, so many tears

We wish that you were still here

The fireplace seems out of place without your stocking

This house seems so strange without you

Baby boy, I know what you been through

God has you free in Heaven

You're dancing on the snow covered road

But it just don't seem like Christmas this year

Down here it's so cold

Merry Christmas in Heaven Garrett

## There's No Friend Like Jesus

There's no friend like Jesus

When I call he answers

When I'm weak, he is strong

If I trust in my friend Jesus

My life will shine

With the gifts he gave me

They are forever mine

There's no other friend like Jesus

He died on the cross for me

What a friend would've taken three nails

Would've taken whips, and death

So we could go to Heaven

And forever rest

Yes, I am a Christian

Yes, I make mistakes

Sometimes I don't pray as much as I should

Only God knows the mistakes I've made

But they made me who I am today

There's no other friend like Jesus

He died on the cross for our sins

So we can live eternal life

## Heaven Must Be Beautiful

Heaven must be beautiful

It has your handsome face

Heaven must be beautiful

A very peaceful place

I know that you're not hurting

I know that you're no-longer in pain

You're cancer free

Just wish that you could call me

Just so I can hear your voice

In heaven had a phone

My cell phone bill would be out of site

But I wouldn't care

Wish that I could fly there

Just if I could visit for a while

We'd sit on a cloud

And talk for a while

I miss you so much

It has been really painful today

I'm running out of words to say

I hope Garrett you know that I got saved

Changed my life around

I hope you're proud

Heaven must be beautiful

It has to be because it has you

Really missing you this Christmas

And days to come

But I'll see you soon

When God calls my name

Meet me at the gate

Stand at the top of the stairs

One day, yes one day I will see you there

## Satan's Going To Have To Deal With Me Being Gone

Satan's going to have to deal with me being gone

I chose to walk with my Lord

On the road of gold

Through a field of flowers

I heard that in Heaven there are no hours

Time doesn't exist there

Satan you never once cared

God and his angels will be waiting

At the top of the stairs

When heaven's gates open wide

Satan you put so much hatred inside me

You knew this depression that I had was real

Satan took the opportunity to steal

Use my nephew's death to take over me

Satan's going to have to deal with me being gone

I'm through with your lies

All the times you made me cry

I chose to walk by God's side on earth

And for eternity in Heaven

## Under Construction Christian

I'm under construction Christian

God's not done with me yet

Still have work that needs to be done

I drove down rocky roads

That wasn't paved

Took detours I should've never took

Didn't take a second look

At the signs God was given me

I'm still an under construction Christian

God has more roads to build for me

And one day I'm going to take that highway

# Broken Soul

One Sunday morning walked through the church doors

Had a broken soul, broken heart

Angry and full of pain

My life had changed

Addiction and destruction had taken over

I walked in the church broken

Didn't care whether or not I lived

Satan had me right where he wanted me

Headed down a tunnel of fire

I had a broken soul, broken dreams

I fell to my knees

At the alter God put his arms around me

Said I'll heal your broken soul

God please help me

I'm breaking again

# Miles To Heaven

I wonder how many miles it is to Heaven

It takes to get to where you are?

I see you in every star

That glows at night in the sky

I still break down and cry

Why did you have to die?

Age 15 to young to go

When I drive your car

I feel you there

People act like to much I care

I remember when you first started to lose your hair

Chemo and radiation took over

It beat you like a punching bag

You grew weak and tired

I wonder how many miles to Heaven

It takes to get where you are

Wish I could jump in your car and drive there

I can't imagine the life you're living today

How shiny is the road of gold?

Have you touched God's face?

Have you met Paul Walker yet?

Has he taught you how to race?

So wish I could see your face

To many miles to Heaven

There's no way there but faith

## Faces Missing In A Frame

This Thanksgiving wasn't the same

Without your faces

Missed you on this this Thanksgiving Day

Can't imagine the party

That you're having with the King

Your faces missing in a picture

Holidays are sad

But we still hold a smile on our face

Miss you Garrett, Tina, and Uncle Jake

Nobody could ever take your place

Faces missing in a picture

We all hold a smile

With the hope God has for us

That we will be reunited once again

And forever be together

## Your Birthday In Heaven

Another year has passed by

And I can't help but wonder why

Why you left before your first breath

But my heart is at comfort

Because I know you're at rest

Another year, year spending your birthday in Heaven

With our Savior Jesus Christ

Walking the golden road right by his side

19 years has went by

I still can't help but wonder why

I wonder what you would've been

Sweet baby boy you had no sins

God took you to the Heavenly light

Your birthday in Heaven

19 years has flew by

We didn't even get to hear your first cry

I know God has his reasons

But still don't understand

Today you'd be such a handsome young man

Who would you be today?

What would you be doing?

What career would you persuading?

Your birthday in Heaven

Another party that I missed

But I'll see you soon baby boy

I'm sending you a kiss to Heaven

Aunt Cookie loves you

## Small Circle Of Friends

You got those friends that's just a text away

You got the fake ones that never stay

When hard times comes your way

You got those friends that stop you

From making some big mistakes

I guess that's the risk you take

When you're down a day

Their just a phone call away

Every day, yes every day

I thank God, the great Lord above

For sending the great ones to say

Don't give up

Yes, I thank him every day

For a small circle of friends

People always say

The more you have

The better off you are

But bigger the group

The harder the fall

All your dreams will hit the wall

The ones you IM at 3 a.m.

Because you can't sleep

You lie awake again

You toss and turn

You can't sleep

Afraid of the dreams the await

Yes, every day, every day

I thank God for a small circle of friends

### God Knows Me So Well

I am weak, but I am strong

In your hands

I can do no wrong

You're there through every storm

You're my thunder, you're my rain

Your lightning strikes within me

God knows me so well

He's there before I am there in life

The sun you shine down is bright

You direct me in the path that's right

God knows me so well

I know I can do anything

When I'm under his care

God knows me so well

When negative people come around

He holds me in his arms safe and sound

I'm blessed to have a friend in Jesus

Who knows my fears, eases my pain

Who's there to comfort me

When I'm going insane

God knows me so well

With his love I can do anything

## When I First See Jesus

When I first see Jesus

First thing I'm going to do

Is thank him, wrap my arms around him

Thank him for helping me get through

There's no friend like Jesus

He knows me more than anyone

He's been there through it all

Whenever I cry

Jesus is by my side

When I first see Jesus

I'll walk the road of gold

And I'll be free

And see my loved ones that's waiting

## Thank God For Tractors

I love to hear the sound

Of my Daddy's John Deere

Driving around this country ground

Big tractors, small town

Everyone gathers when something bad goes down

Farming the country farm

We don't use firearms

We use tractors and Chevy trucks

During hunting season the hunters go for a big buck

Thank God for tractors

Thank God for country roads

They'll lead you anywhere you want to go

Hit pot holes

I love the feeling in my soul

Five years ago I made a big mistake

Left the country, moved to a different place

Seen new faces, fell to my knees

But I had to fall to find me

Home is where the heart is

South Webster, Ohio I will die here

Thank God for tractors

Thank God for pickup trucks

Thank God for the fishing holes

And the fishing poles

Country dirt on the ground

Our basketball team went State Bound

In 2004, was the night the Jeeps ruled the court

Thank God for tractors

Thank God for family that isn't blood

We ride 4-wheelers through the mud

Thank God for South Webster

Thank God for bringing me home

## Until We Meet Again

The wind blows softly through the trees

You're sending down your love

Through the summer breeze

It's been almost a year, and still you're missed

To see you again, what we would give

This small town is still the same

But yet it's quiet when we hear your name

We hear you at night at the bonfires

We think of you when the sun rises

We feel you in the sunset

What are you doing in Heaven?

Matthew Roy we'll see you soon

You will be forever in our hearts

Until' we meet again

Made in the USA
Columbia, SC
20 October 2024

44781405R00024